Piano I

SCHIRMER'S LIBRARY
OF MUSICAL CLASSICS

Vol. 1619

CORNELIUS GURLITT

Op. 174

Eight
Melodious Pieces

For Two Pianos, Four-Hands

ISBN 0-7935-4950-7

G. SCHIRMER, Inc.

DISTRIBUTED BY

HAL•LEONARD®
CORPORATION
7777 W. BLUEMOUND RD. P.O. BOX 13819 MILWAUKEE, WI 53213

Eight Melodious Pieces

Piano I.

Allegretto scherzando.

C. Gurlitt, Op. 174

1.

Piano I.

Moderato.

2.

Piano I.

Moderato.

Piano I.

3.

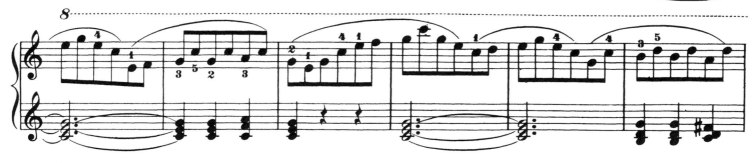

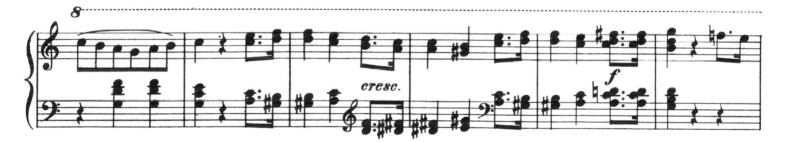

Piano I.

4.

Con moto energico.

5.

f risoluto

Piano II

SCHIRMER'S LIBRARY
OF MUSICAL CLASSICS

Vol. 1619

CORNELIUS GURLITT

Op. 174

Eight
Melodious Pieces

For Two Pianos, Four-Hands

ISBN 0-7935-4950-7

G. SCHIRMER, Inc.

DISTRIBUTED BY
HAL•LEONARD®
CORPORATION
7777 W. BLUEMOUND RD. P.O. BOX 13819 MILWAUKEE, WI 53213

Eight Melodious Pieces

Piano II.

C. Gurlitt, Op. 174

Allegretto scherzando.

1.

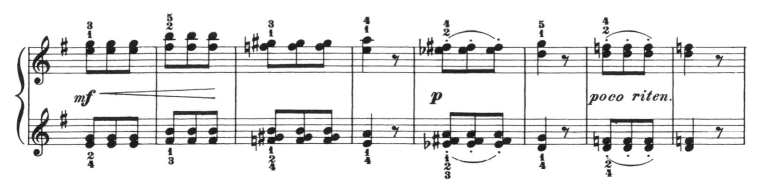

Piano II.

Moderato.

2.

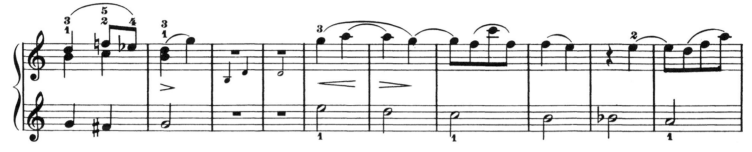

Piano II.

Moderato.

3.

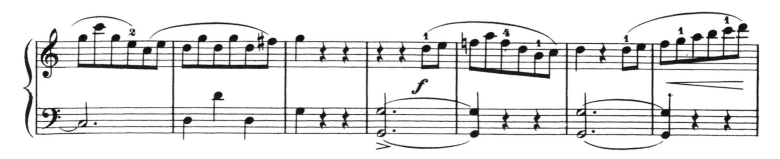

Piano II.

4.

Piano II.

Con moto energico.

Moderato, tempo di Gavotta.

6.

Piano II.

Allegretto. (Hunting Scene.)

7.

Piano II.

Allegretto, tempo di Valse.

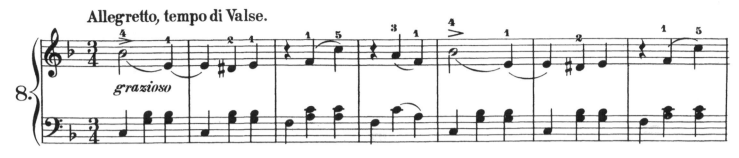

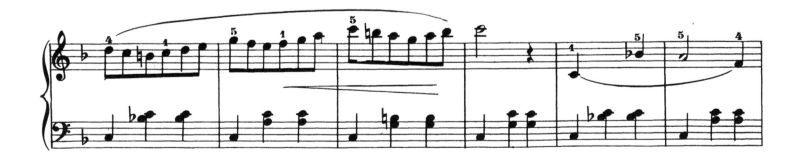

Piano II.

Piano II.

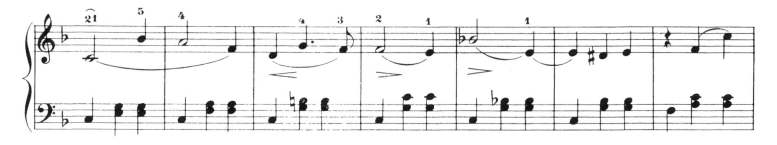

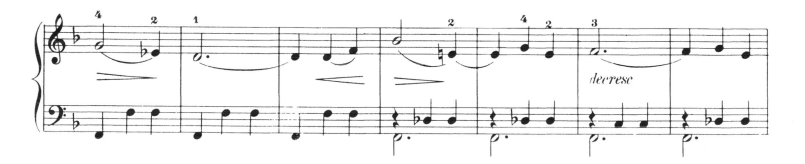

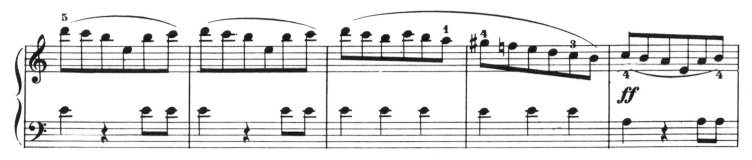

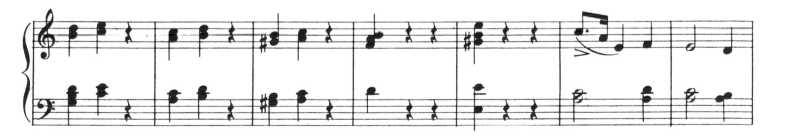

Piano I.

Moderato, tempo di Gavotta.

marcato

6.

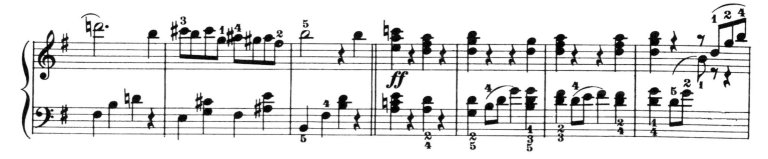

cantabile

Piano I.

Allegretto. (Hunting Scene.)

7.

Piano I.

Piano I.

Allegretto, tempo di Valse.

8.

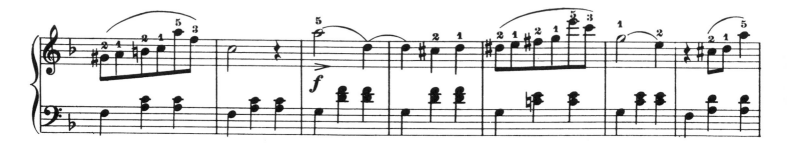

Piano I.

Piano I.

Piano I.